1ST BIRTHDAY SPECIAL SOUVENIR

CONTENTS

06 THE FIRST BIRTHDAY

14 THE EARLY DAYS

20 THE CHRISTENING

28 FIRST YEAR AS MUM AND DAD

42 THE ROYAL YEAR

48 ROYALS AGED 1

54 GROWING UP IN PUBLIC

58 GEORGE DOWN UNDER

72 A NATION'S PRIDE

HRH Prince George

![Mirror Collection]

A Mirror publication

Head of Syndication & Licensing: Fergus McKenna

Mirrorpix: David Scripps, Simon Flavin

020 7293 3858

Produced by Trinity Mirror Media

PO BOX 48, Liverpool, L69 3EB

Managing Director: Ken Rogers

Publishing Director: Steve Hanrahan

Executive Art Editor: Rick Cooke

Senior Editor: Paul Dove

Produced by: Roy Gilfoyle

Written by: Chris Brereton

Designed by: Lee Ashun

Part of the Mirror Collection

© Published by Trinity Mirror 2014

Images: Mirrorpix, PA Photos

Printed by William Gibbons

MONDAY 16.06.2014 DAILY MIRROR 3

mirror.co.uk

GRAND STAND George takes a few steps with help from Kate yesterday

Prince George is stepping up ...for England

Tot has kickabout with Kate

BY **VICTORIA MURPHY** Royal Reporter

PRINCE George is a right little Royal of the Rovers as he kicks a football with help from doting mum Kate.

The 11-month-old tot took his first steps in public yesterday as he showed the England team how it's done with a kickabout.

George spent the afternoon toddling around with number one supporter Kate, 32, supplying a helping hand as his dad William, 31, and uncle Harry, 29, played in an annual charity polo match in Cirencester, Glos.

The future King, who will be one on July 22, kept himself – and mum – busy crawling, chewing things, grabbing polo mallets and staring at the horses.

On the spring royal tour to New Zealand and Australia other first-time parents who met George described him as "advanced", "feisty" and "intrepid".

And the boisterous prince showed he's still progressing well as he took several steps, holding just one of his mummy's hands.

George, who has not been seen in public since his return from Down Under in April, was dressed in a summery red and white romper suit with a white shirt and black shoes and socks.

Stylish Kate looked casual in skinny jeans and nautical blue and white Breton striped top.

Today Kate and William will leave George at home with his Spanish nanny to join the Queen and other royals attending the annual Order of the Garter Service at Windsor Castle.

victoria.murphy@mirror.co.uk

KISS Kate backs Wills

FOOTMAN Royal George kicks ball on grass

THEY DRINK IT'S ALL OVER Dad Wills gives tot some water

I WANT MY BAWL BACK George looks set to cry

MORE GREAT PICTURES mirror.co.uk

A Year
AS THE NATION'S
DARLING

From his historic birth to his first steps…

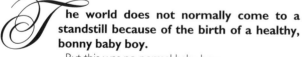

'The clamour and interest in George's young life shows no signs of slowing down'

The world does not normally come to a standstill because of the birth of a healthy, bonny baby boy.

But this was no normal baby boy.

Born at 4.42pm on July 22, 2013, George Alexander Louis, also known as Prince George of Cambridge, was born in the Lindo Wing of St Mary's Hospital, London.

And so the country, sweltering on the hottest day for seven years, and the world, could finally rejoice.

The wait was over – Prince William, Duke of Cambridge and George's mother, Catherine, Duchess of Cambridge, could celebrate the birth of their first child.

The event well and truly dominated the nation's thoughts and overshadowed everything else.

The sporting world had been awash with success as Andy Murray had ended Britain's long wait for a Wimbledon champion and there was further British glory in golf's US Open thanks to Justin Rose as well as Chris Froome's awesome Tour de France victory.

In other royal news, the remains of Richard III were discovered buried in a car park in Leicester and the Queen had a controversial new portrait painted by Dan Llywelyn Hall.

But no event was going to kick Prince George and his ➤

He may look like any ordinary, happy baby, playing with his toys, but this could be the future King of the United Kingdom

mum and dad off the front pages or off the airwaves.

Prince George's birth was a truly historic moment. The Queen became the first living monarch to see a great-grandchild born in direct succession since Queen Victoria 120 years previously and the little boy's arrival meant that the monarchy had three generations of heirs to the throne for the first time since 1901.

Now that Prince George has reached his first birthday, the clamour and interest in his young life shows no signs of slowing down.

And he has had an action-packed first 12 months.

Although Prince George has largely been shielded from public glare, he has already begun his globetrotting thanks to an official trip to Australia and New Zealand, where he captured the hearts and minds of an adoring public.

Held in high regard

Left and below: **Mummy clutches her first-born**

Bottom: **Kate accepts a gift for her son**

Prince George is stepping up ...for England

Tot has kickabout with Kate

BY **VICTORIA MURPHY**
Royal Reporter

PRINCE George is a right little Royal of the Rovers as he kicks a football with help from doting mum Kate.

The 11-month-old tot took his first steps in public yesterday as he showed the England team how it's done with a kickabout.

George spent the afternoon toddling around with number one supporter Kate, 32, supplying a helping hand as his dad William, 31, and uncle Harry, 29, played in an annual charity polo match in Cirencester, Glos.

The future King, who will be one on July 22, kept himself – and mum – busy crawling, chewing things, grabbing polo mallets and staring at the horses.

On the spring royal tour to New Zealand and Australia other first-time parents who met George described him as "advanced", "feisty" and "intrepid".

KISS Kate backs Wills

And the boisterous prince showed he's still progressing well as he took several steps, holding just one of his mummy's hands.

George, who has not been seen in public since his return from Down Under in April, was dressed in a summery red and white romper suit with a white shirt and black shoes and socks.

Stylish Kate looked casual in skinny jeans and nautical blue and white Breton striped top.

Today Kate and William will leave George at home with his Spanish nanny to join the Queen and other royals attending the annual Order of the Garter Service at Windsor Castle.

victoria.murphy@mirror.co.uk

FOOTMAN Royal George kicks ball on grass

THEY DRINK IT'S ALL OVER Dad Wills gives tot some water

MORE GREAT PICTURES mirror.co.uk

I WANT MY BAWL BACK George looks set to cry

The first pictures of Prince George walking – and even playing football – were captured in the Daily Mirror in June 2014

When they do appear as a family, the Prince and Princess of Cambridge seem happy to show their son off to the world.

George has been pictured playing with other babies in nurseries and he's been photographed crying, hugging his mum and doing everything else a healthy, happy baby boy does.

He has also recently been photographed taking a few steps, showing that he is developing well under the guidance of two doting parents.

He is set for an incredible life of privilege and power in front of a passionate public.

So let's remember, celebrate and enjoy Prince George and the first year of what will undoubtedly be a remarkable life.

'Let's celebrate the first year of what will undoubtedly be a remarkable life'

Prince George gets used to the 'meet and greet' on the first day of his tour to Australia and New Zealand

The waiting public in New Zealand show how happy they are to see William, Kate and George

A Royal ARRIVAL

A national obsession begins...

The enormous press packs sweltered in the heat. Reporters tried their best to fill hours and hours or airtime.

Gossip flew through the air and rumours were rife about if, when and how the Princess of Cambridge had given birth.

But, finally, at 8.29pm on July 22, a spokesperson for Clarence House announced in a press release that Prince George had been safely born.

All of a sudden, those same reporters and TV crews had cast-iron happy news to deliver to a world that was hanging off every word.

Prince George had arrived.

However, the action had really begun 14 hours earlier – when George first made clear that the time was here for him to be born.

At 6am, the Duke and Duchess of Cambridge arrived at St Mary's Hospital, Paddington, London, using a back entrance to the Lindo Wing so they could avoid the hundreds of media people present.

Almost two hours later, Kensington Palace finally confirmed that Kate Middleton had gone into labour and that everything was going nicely to plan.

Twitter, Facebook and news channels around the world went into meltdown, especially in the heat, as celebrities ranging from Piers Morgan to John Prescott wished the royal couple luck on the most important day of their lives.

Prime Minister David Cameron then joined in before Prince Charles, visiting the National Railway Museum in York, let slip to a member of the public that he had no idea what was happening. "I know absolutely nothing at the moment," he told a member of the public, "we're just waiting to find out."

As lunchtime arrived, thousands of well-wishers started to gather at Buckingham Palace as it became clear that today was the day.

It was a long afternoon as the public and press waited for something to be announced but behind the closed doors of the Lindo Wing, the Princess of Cambridge was doing all the hard work, until, at 4.24pm, Prince George was born.

Rumours continued to circulate around the world until that Clarence House press release gave the public the green light to start celebrating.

The announcement of Prince George's arrival via a press release was a very modern and savvy way of delivering the news to the world.

However, the Royal Family are also sticklers for history and tradition and they were not going to miss this opportunity.

As a result, at 8.48pm, a traditional easel, on which royal births had always previously been announced, was placed in the grounds of Buckingham Palace by Badar Azim, a footman with the Royal Household, and Ailsa Anderson, the Queen's press secretary, for the public to read.

The press pack set up outside St Mary's Hospital

Kate gazes adoringly at her new baby

Daily Mirror front pages in the days after George's birth

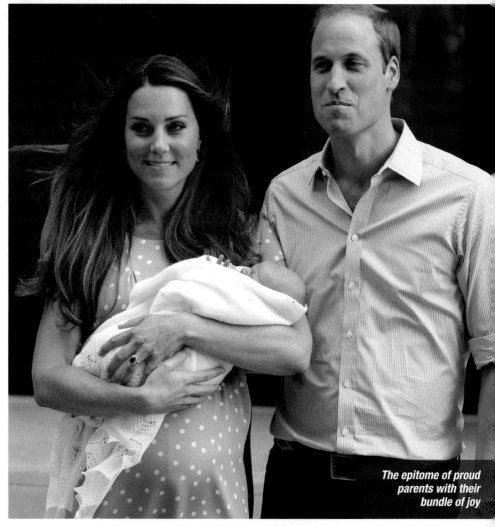

The epitome of proud parents with their bundle of joy

*Above and left:
William carefully
carries his new son
while the gathered
crowds and media
get their first glimpse
of the royal arrival*

As night falls people are still gathered at Buckingham Palace where an easel was placed to announce the arrival of a new royal baby on July 22, 2013

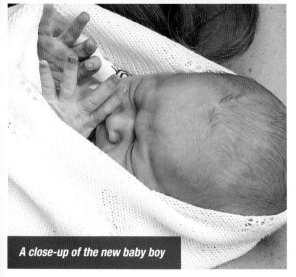

A close-up of the new baby boy

A family photo taken at the home of Kate's parents in August 2013

To mark the birth, the London Eye was lit up red, white and blue and the BT Tower and Trafalgar Square were also illuminated.

The day after the birth, Prince Charles and Camilla visited the baby along with Kate's parents, Carole and Michael.

They all emerged from the hospital with huge smiles on their faces — but that was nothing compared to the grins shared by William and Kate when they too showed up on the steps of the Lindo Wing to show off their new son.

"It's very emotional," Kate told reporters. "It's such a special time. I think any parent will know what this feels like."

Prince William was in a playful mood with the media and joked that he was glad his son, who weighed 8lb 6oz at birth, had his mother's looks.

"He's got a good pair of lungs on him, that's for sure," he added. "He's a big boy, he's quite heavy."

And with that, William placed his son in his car seat and drove his wife and newborn away from hospital and into their new lives.

It was two days later that the name of the new prince was announced by Kensington Palace. George Alexander Louis were the names chosen meaning he would also be referred to as His Royal Highness Prince George of Cambridge.

The public's love affair with Prince George had well and truly begun.

Above: A fan of the Royal Family camps out to wait for the new arrival

Right: William looks down on his son

A *Quiet* CHRISTENING

The chosen few see prince baptised in replica gown

Very few events in the lives of the Royal Family are quiet, intimate affairs. However, Prince George's christening was exactly that.

Only 22 guests attended the service in the Chapel Royal at St James's Palace in London. It was an occasion for senior royals only as well as four members of the Middleton family.

The Archbishop of Canterbury conducted the service, watched by Prince George's godparents; Oliver Baker, Emilia Jardine-Paterson, Earl Grosvenor, Jamie Lowther-Pinkerton, Julia Samuel, William van Cutsem and Zara Tindall.

Zara Tindall is, of course, Prince William's cousin, while the other godparents are all friends of William and Kate.

It was particularly poignant to see Julia Samuel as a godparent as she was very close to William's mother Diana, Princess of Wales, while Jamie Lowther-Pinkerton is a former aide to William and has helped to prepare him for when he becomes King.

For the 45-minute ceremony William and Kate chose two hymns, two lessons and two anthems for the christening.

The hymns were *Breathe on Me, Breath of God* and *Be Thou My Vision*.

Lessons from St Luke and St John were read by Pippa Middleton and Prince Harry, and the anthems were *Blessed Jesus! Here We Stand* and *Lord Bless You and Keep You*.

The anthems were sung by the Choir of Her Majesty's Chapel Royal, which performed at the royal couple's wedding, and once the ceremony was finished, Prince George left the Chapel Royal in the arms of Kate as they headed off for tea at Clarence House.

George's outfit for his christening caused quite a stir – and rightly so!

On just his second public appearance – the first being on the steps of the Lindo Wing the day after his birth – George wore a replica of the original Royal Christening Gown.

The original version was designed in 1841 for Queen Victoria's eldest daughter, Victoria, the Princess Royal.

In the years since then, over 60 Royals were christened in the gown but its age and increasing fragility meant it can no longer be worn.

However, all was not lost as the Queen asked her couturier, Angela Kelly, to craft a hand-made replica version in 2008.

Prince George might have stolen the show in the gown but he was not the first to wear the replica garment.

That accolade goes to James, Viscount Severn, who wore it at his christening at Windsor Castle in April, 2008.

Clockwise from top:

Kate and William take turns carrying George

The Queen and Duke of Edinburgh chat to the Archbishop of Canterbury

William and Kate look relaxed as they arrive for George's big day

Selected guests arrive for Prince George's christening

Celebrating with
The Prince & Duchess of Cambridge the
Christening of Prince George
at
Chapel Royal St James

William, Kate, George and the Archbishop of Canterbury

Royal enthusiasts gather outside St James' Palace

Prince George

Congratulations Prince George on your Christening

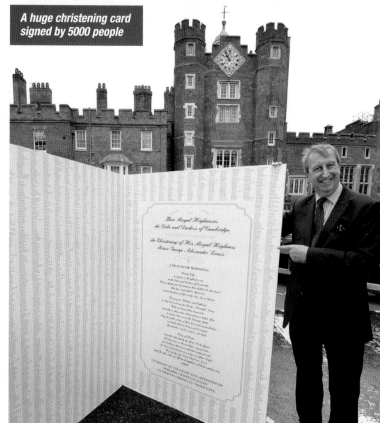

A huge christening card signed by 5000 people

'Only 22 guests attended the service. It was an occasion for senior royals only as well as four members of the Middleton family'

Kate beams with pride as she holds George after the christening ceremony, which was attended by Prince Harry (left)

KEEPING A SPECIAL OCCASION ALIVE

One thing can be guaranteed whenever there is a Royal birth, christening, wedding or funeral. Memorabilia will be churned out left, right and centre.

A quick peek online will show the weird and wonderful trinkets available to those wanting to remember a royal event.

For George's birth and christening, mugs, tea towels, DVDs, a tableware set and a commemorative medal were all available and around the country, souvenir shops noted record sales of keyrings, Prince George-embossed souvenir plates and a whole host of other memorabilia.

A Gold Proof Kilo Coin (left) and Silver Proof Kilo Coin (right) were struck to celebrate Prince George's christening

Queen Elizabeth II was christened in Buckingham Palace's private chapel

A BREAK FROM TRADITION

George becomes first future monarch in recent times to be christened away from Buckingham Palace

The chance to catch up with friends, family and loved ones and celebrate a great day. Who doesn't love a good christening?

The Royal Family are no different.

Christenings are an important spiritual and social occasion for the Royal Family, especially as Prince George will one day carry the title 'Defender of the Faith and Supreme Governor of the Church of England'.

George is the first future monarch in modern times not to be baptised at Buckingham Palace with both his dad, William, and grandfather, Charles, christened in the palace's Music Room.

The Queen, who was not expected to be Queen when born, was christened in the Palace's private chapel in 1926.

Edward VIII, who later abdicated, was baptised at White Lodge in Richmond Park in 1894 and his brother George VI, who was not expected to be King, was christened at the Church of St Mary Magdalene close to the Sandringham estate in 1895.

William was baptised on August 4, 1982, at the age of six weeks, while the Prince of Wales was one month and one day old at his own christening.

The Queen was just over five weeks old when she was christened.

Princess Eugenie, Prince Andrew and the Duchess of York's daughter, was the first royal baby to have a public christening as she was baptised during morning service at the church of St Mary Magdalene at Sandringham just before Christmas in 1990.

Most royal christenings have gone to plan – but they've not always been plain sailing.

At Queen Victoria's in 1819, there was a dispute over what she should be called.

Her mother, the Duchess of Kent, had wanted to call her Georgiana Charlotte Augusta Alexandrina Victoria, but was overruled by a cantankerous Prince Regent, the future George IV, who dictated during the ceremony that she be called Alexandrina Victoria instead in tribute to the Russian Tsar Alexander I.

The Duchess was left distraught and broke down sobbing during the proceedings.

However, there were no such problems at George's christening as he left the church alongside his delighted parents.

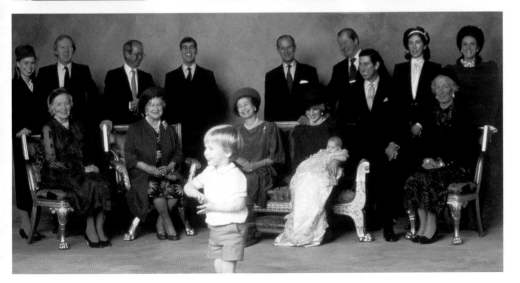

Babes in arms

Top: *Prince Charles and Prince William were christened in Buckingham Palace's Music Room*

Middle left: *Princess Eugenie was the first royal baby to have a public christening*

Middle right: *Princess Anne with son Peter*

Left: *William steals the show at brother Harry's christening photo*

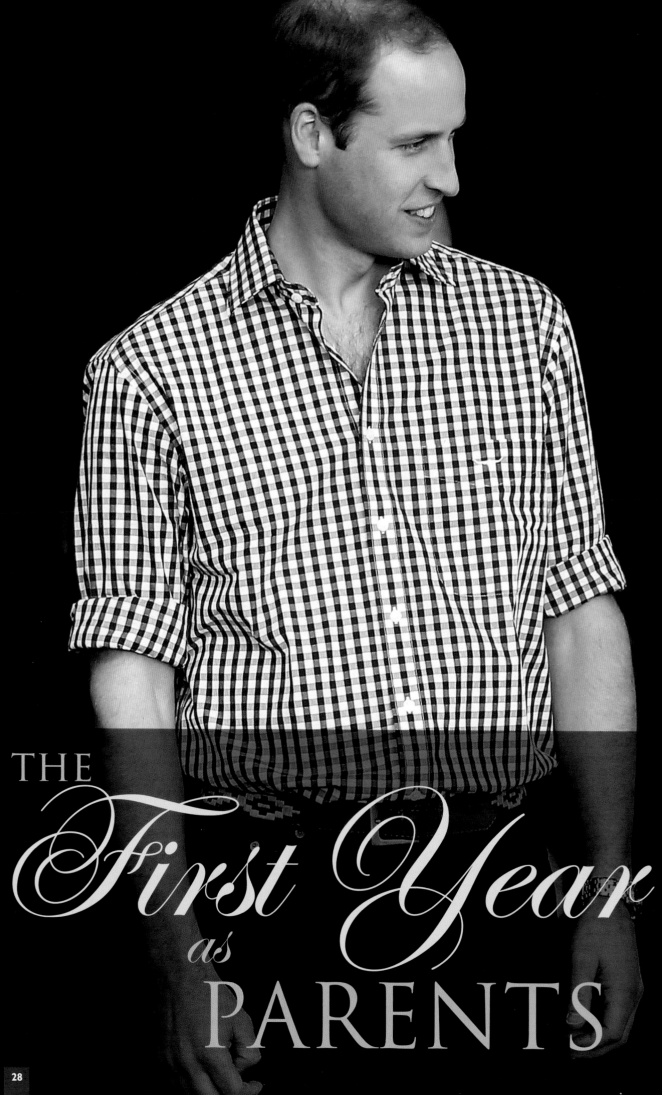

THE *First Year* as PARENTS

A heavily pregnant Kate at a ship-naming ceremony in Southampton – her last public appearance before giving birth

KATE CAREFUL TO GIVE GEORGE A 'NORMAL' UPBRINGING

As with every mother across the globe, Kate Middleton's first days, weeks and months with her newborn baby made for special moments.

However, most of those took place well and truly behind closed doors.

Following Prince George's much-snapped exit from the Lindo Wing, the young prince was rarely seen in public as William and Kate took time out to get to know their new son.

Throughout her pregnancy and following the birth, Kate has made it crystal clear that she wanted to be as 'normal' as possible and see George as often as other mothers see their children.

Being a child born into the Royal Family usually means a coterie of nurses and nannies bring you up but Kate never wanted that – and it showed.

Kate and William had been expected to attend the society wedding of James Meade and Lady Laura Marsham, daughter of the Earl of Romney just six weeks after George's birth but in the end, William attended on his own, with rumours circulating that Kate preferred to stay at home and out of the limelight as she cared for her six-week-old son.

Generally speaking, Kate's first 12 months following the birth of George have been relatively low key. Apart from the three-week tour of Australia and New Zealand, both Kate and George have remained practically unseen.

Before the birth of Prince George, Kate's last public

Kate has continued with her public appearances, but kept them to a minimum since becoming a mum

'Apart from a few events Kate and George have remained under the radar, further proof that the modern day Royal Family are doing all they can to ensure George has a normal, happy childhood'

engagement was attending a ship naming ceremony at Ocean Terminal, Southampton, on June 13 and she remained out of the public eye until she joined William at the Ring O' Fire Anglesey Coastal Ultra Marathon in August.

After that, public appearances have continued to be strictly rationed.

Kate joined William at the inaugural Tusk Conservation Awards at The Royal Society, London, in September before just a handful of other public appearances in 2013.

2014 has followed the same pattern with Kate attending events at Northolt High School, Ealing, and the National Portrait Gallery in February, while the early part of the summer was taken up with a June event at the National Maritime Musuem in Greenwich as well as the Tour De France Grand Depart in Yorkshire on July 5.

However, apart from those events, Kate and George have remained under the radar and that is further proof that the modern day Royal Family – unlike in earlier times – are doing all they can to ensure that Prince George can have a normal, happy and healthy childhood.

The fact that Kate and George have been out of the public eye is also down to the stresses and strains of moving house.

In the Autumn of 2013, Prince William and his family moved into a 21-room apartment inside Kensington Palace. The apartment was Princess Margaret's former residence but has been upgraded to ensure a newborn child can be safely brought up there. Kate oversaw and organised a huge amount of the move and that also restricted her public commitments.

Out and about

Top left: Kate receives a cuddly corgi from a well-wisher in Crieff, Scotland

Above left: The happy couple watch a rugby tournament in Dunedin, New Zealand

Above: Kate tries her hand at volleyball at the Copper Box in the Olympic Park, London

Left: Kate goes for the nautical look as she meets the public of Auckland, New Zealand, then pitches in on board a boat

HAPPY PARENTS CALL IN THE BABYSITTERS

Kate's first public appearance after the birth of Prince George came at the Holyhead Breakwater Country Park as she joined Prince William in starting the Ring O' Fire Anglesey Coastal Ultra Marathon.

The event is a gruelling 135-mile run that circumnavigates the whole of the island of Anglesey.

Kate mingled happily with the runners and those watching the tiring event and she told the waiting crowd that her own mother, Carole, was on babysitting duties.

"George is doing very well. He's with granny at the moment. He's sleeping well but I know these things suddenly change," she said.

Kate and William looked super relaxed at the event and could feel at home in the area as they lived in a rented farmhouse in North Wales.

They have since moved to Kensington Palace but retain close links with Anglesey and North Wales in general.

Kate and William at the Holyhead Breakwater Country Park in North Wales in August 2013

William talks to a young girl in New Zealand

William went back to school to study agricultural management at Cambridge University

BACK TO WORK FOR A 21ST CENTURY DAD

As is the case in most families, while mum Kate stayed out of the limelight with Prince George, dad Prince William returned to his job and his duties relatively quickly and the Royal merry-go-round of engagements and appointments ensured the public saw plenty of the new father.

In 2013, William conducted 18 public engagements following the birth of George and his duties ranged from handing out Operational Service Medals, for deployment in Afghanistan, to soldiers of No. 2 Company, 1st Battalion Irish Guards to attending the UK premiere of Mandela: Long Walk to Freedom, at the Odeon Leicester Square, London.

2014 has been equally as hectic, especially as it was announced that William would also be attending Cambridge University for a 10-week course in agricultural management; a move designed to help him take a hands-on role when he inherits the Duchy of Cornwall estate from his father.

This year, William and Kate, known as the Earl and Countess of Strathearn in Scotland, have toured Perth and Kinross as well as embarking on their three-week tour of Australia and New Zealand together – although the star of the show Down Under was Prince George, rather than his royal parents.

William, as second in line to the throne, automatically has more duties and engagements than his wife but he often demonstrated and spoke of his desire and willingness to help raise Prince George as much as possible.

He may be a very busy man but he is also the epitome of a 21st century dad. He wants to be there and he wants to help.

And although he may have to clock up the air miles as part of his royal role, William looks certain to play a huge and defining role in his son's life – just as Prince Charles has done with William himself.

'Although he may have to clock up the air miles as part of his royal role, William looks certain to play a huge and defining role in his son's life'

Kate and William on their first overseas tour with their son in Australia and New Zealand

Joining in story time with children at a new library in Birmingham

Public engagements are still part of William's role

William takes on investiture duties at Buckingham Palace

MARIA'S SPECIAL ROLE

Maria Borrallo (top) and Prince William's press secretary Miguel Head arrive in New Zealand

Despite their insistence on being as hands-on as possible, it would be virtually impossible for William and Kate to cope without a nanny.

The sheer amount of public engagements and responsibilities the couple share mean that employing a nanny was a formality rather than something out of the norm.

The couple chose Spanish nanny Maria Teresa Turrion Borrallo for the job and she first accompanied William, Kate and George on the trip to Australia and New Zealand.

Ms Borrallo trained at Norland College which had produced nannies and childminders since 1892.

The college is not cheap and training costs over £30,000 for a three-year course.

Kate's mum, Carole Middleton, has also been regularly enlisted as a helper while William's own former nanny Jessie Webb has also taken on babysitting duties from time to time.

However, no matter how dedicated Ms Borrallo is to her job, William and Kate seem determined to raise George as much – and as often – as their daunting schedules allow.

Maria Borrallo is always on hand – as she was here at Government House in Wellington, New Zealand

GEORGE'S FIRST

Royal

YEAR

We know he's been busy learning how to eat, walk and look cute, but we hope George had enough time to keep an eye on the rest of the family so he knows what duties lie in store in the years ahead

Although the birth of Prince George sent the international media into meltdown, his celebrated arrival was by no means the only major event to involve the Royal Family over the past year.

It has, in a lot of ways been business as usual – although several events have well and truly stood out.

While most great-grandmothers would have the chance to sit down with their newborn great-grandchild, the Queen was straight back to the day job just 24 hours after Prince George was born. She hosted a reception for the winners of the Queens Award for Enterprise 2013 at Buckingham Palace in London where she met business leaders, young and old, before she then headed to Balmoral for the summer, where she inspected various troops, including the Royal Scots Borderers.

As well as watching the Trooping of the Colour and her annual visits to both Parliament for its State Opening and also Royal Ascot, the Queen also made headlines for hosting a banquet in April for the President of the Republic of Ireland, Michael Higgins – a meal at Windsor that also saw former IRA commander Martin McGuinness present, in a mutual bid to ease the memory of the horrors of The Troubles in Northern Ireland.

The Queen also represented the United Kingdom at the poignant 70th anniversary of the D-Day landings in June this year, while in April she went to the Vatican to visit Pope Francis.

Prince Philip slowed down for most of 2013 as the 93-year-old recovered from surgery on his abdomen in June but since then, whenever possible, he has taken his place next to the Queen and continued the unstinting

'The Queen represented the UK at the 70th anniversary of the D-Day landings and also went to the Vatican to meet Pope Francis'

support he has shown her for over 60 years.

The Duke remains the patron of nearly 800 charities and organisations so his diary has been as crammed as ever, accompanying the Queen to events in Scotland as well as also being in Normandy for the D-Day commemorations.

The Prince of Wales and Duchess of Cornwall have shown no signs of slowing down their own public engagements either since the birth of Prince George.

Charles and Camilla visited George in hospital but have since got back to their usual roles of representing the military and fighting for a whole host of different causes, from Prince Charles' well-known love of agriculture and his attempts to protect the British countryside to Camilla's own interests in preventing osteoporosis, a bone-thinning disease that badly affected her own mother.

The Prince of Wales and Duchess of Cornwall have undertaken hundreds of public openings and events in the past 12 months.

They visited Normandy to show their respects to the Allied serviceman who stormed the beaches in 1944 and they also both toured Canada in May.

And perhaps the highest profile 'job' was the Duchess of Cornwall's meeting with Hollywood superstar Angelina Jolie in June, 2014, as she attended the global summit to 'End Sexual Violence in Conflict' that was held in London.

Prince Harry has also had a typically busy 12 months since he became an uncle.

He has visited Italy, Estonia, Brazil and Chile, among other places, and he's also attended events as diverse as the 50th Anniversary Premiere of the film Zulu and the commemoration service for former South African President, Nelson Mandela.

Prince Harry is always extremely keen to show his respect to wounded servicemen and women from the Armed Forces and he's also attended many events showing his support for former soldiers, sailors and aimen.

The Duchess of Cornwall with Angelina Jolie while promoting a campaign to end sexual violence in war zones

Prince Harry joins in a game of sit down volleyball with soldiers at the Warrior Games

Prince Charles meets American president Barack Obama while in Normandy to mark the 70th anniversary of the D-Day landings

THE STORIES THAT HIT THE HEADLINES IN GEORGE'S FIRST YEAR

August 2013
5: The world's first laboratory-grown burger is cooked and eaten at a news conference in London.
29: The House of Commons defeats the Government motion backing military intervention in Syria by 285 votes to 272.

September 2013
3: The Library of Birmingham, the largest public library in the UK, is opened.
10: MP Nigel Evans resigns as a Deputy Speaker of the House of Commons after being charged with sexual offences. He was later cleared in court.

October 2013
7: Launch of the National Crime Agency.
26: The Rugby League World Cup began.

November 2013
14: The last living British person to be born in the 1800s, Grace Jones, dies at the age of 113.
29: Eight people are killed and 19 seriously injured after a police helicopter crashes into The Clutha pub in Glasgow.

December 2013
19: Part of the ceiling of the Apollo Theatre in London collapses during a performance.
23: World War II computer pioneer and codebreaker Alan Turing, who had been chemically castrated in 1952 following his conviction for homosexuality, is given a posthumous royal pardon.

January 2014
3: Large parts of Britain are brought to a standstill by wet weather and severe flooding.
18: 16-year-old Lewis Clarke sets a new world record after becoming the youngest person to trek to the South Pole.

Royal duties

Clockwise, from right:

The Queen signs a message to go in the Glasgow 2014 Commonwealth Games baton

A Buckingham Palace garden party on the Duke of Edinburgh's birthday in June

Prince Charles wields a mallet on an offical trip to Canada

Prince William awards tennis star Andy Murray an OBE at Buckingham Palace

A Windsor Castle parade during the Irish president Michael D Higgins' historic state visit

The Queen and the Duke of Edinburgh at the state opening of Parliament

BY GEORGE, LOOK AT THOSE NAMES

Michael Buble & Luisana Lopilato

Celebrity babies born in George's first year

July 22: **Luna** (Penelope Cruz and Javier Bardem)
August 7: **Vernon Lindsay** (Vince Vaughn & Kyla Weber)
August 12: **Jett** (Katie Price and Kieran Hayler)
August 27: **Noah** (Michael Buble and Luisana Lopilato)
September 13: **Elsie** (Ioan Gruffudd and Alice Evans)
October 5: **Maceo** (Halle Berry and Olivier Martinez)
November 8: **Luka Violet Toni** (Holly Valance and Nick Candy)
December 7: **Bear** (Kate Winslet and Ned Rocknroll)
January 17: **Mia Grace** (Mike Tindall and Zara Phillips)
February 14: **Eric** (Simon Cowell and Lauren Silverman)
February 28: **Apollo Bowie Flynn** (Gwen Stefani and Gavin Rossdale)
April 11: **Sunday Molly** (Mike Myers and Kelly Tisdale)
April 17: **Winston** (Idris Elba and Naiyana Garth)
April 22: **Frankie** (Drew Barrymore and Will Kopelman)
May 6: **Leo and Lenny** (twins to Roger Federer and Mirka Vavrinec)

Simon Cowell & Lauren Silverman

THE STORIES THAT HIT THE HEADLINES IN GEORGE'S FIRST YEAR

February 2014
7–23: Great Britain wins one gold, one silver and two bronze medals at the Winter Olympic Games in Sochi, Russia.

March 2014
29: The first gay weddings take place in England and Wales.
31: A jury is selected to hear a fresh inquest into the 1989 Hillsborough disaster.

April 2014
5: In horse racing, Pineau De Re wins the 2014 Grand National.
22: David Moyes is sacked as manager of Manchester United after just 10 months.

May 2014
23: A major fire damages the Glasgow School of Art.
24: Jonny Wilkinson retires from rugby union after helping Toulon beat Saracens 23–6 in the Heineken Cup final.

June 2014
9: Comedy actor and writer Rik Mayall dies.
12: The England national football team competes at the World Cup in Brazil.

Katie Price & Kieran Hayler

Holly Valance & Nick Candy

Kate Winslet

When ONE *turns* ONE

We know George is a cute one-year-old, but what did his relatives look like around the same age. Here are a few of them...

When the Duchess of Cambridge walked down the steps of the Airbus A380 that had taken her, Prince William and their son to New Zealand, for the first time since she married into the Royal Family three years ago, she was not the centre of attention.

Dressed in a dashing red outfit and with a New Zealand fern brooch pinned to her lapel, the paparazzi present would normally have gone into overdrive about how glamorous and beautiful she looked, especially after a marathon flight around the world.

However, on that occasion, all eyes were on Prince George.

And everybody present – and everybody who devoured the coverage in print or online in the coming days – all said the same thing: "Isn't Prince George the double of his father?"

The likeness between father and son is unmistakable.

When Prince Wiliam was a one-year-old, he was a cheery, smiley, bonny boy with a shock of blond hair and chubby cheeks.

And Prince George is his spitting image. Well maybe not quite, according to dad who has quipped that Prince George "has way more hair than me."

It would appear that Prince George also shares his dad's mischievous spirit.

"He's a little bit of a rascal," Prince William continued.

"He's growing quite quickly now and he's a little fighter, he wriggles around a lot."

When William's own father, Prince Charles, was born in 1948, church bells rang up and down the country as the then Princess Elizabeth delivered a son who will one day sit on the throne.

It was thought for a long time that Prince Charles and the Queen did not have a particularly close relationship when he was a child because of her preparations to take over as Queen. Her father, King George VI, was ill for a sustained period and it seemed inevitable that the young Princess would become the monarch sooner rather than later. That meant Charles was cared for by a host of nannies rather than his parents. However, recently-revealed footage has shown that the Queen loved spending time with her eldest

George's dad William in a garden at Kensington Palace with his parents as he approached the 18-month mark

child, who also carried the distinctive Windsor look that has been passed on to William, Harry and now Prince George.

In fact, it appears to be a common family trait that male members of the Windsor family all look nearly identical after 12 months!

Prince George is blond, bonny, playful and smiley. His dad was the same – and so was his grandad!

When Princess Anne was born in 1950, Prince Andrew in 1960 and Prince Andrew in 1964, the distinctive family look continued.

All the Queen's children were blond and happy – and Prince George has carried that on.

In fact, when it comes to looks, the only real quirk in the recent Royal Family tree has been Prince Harry.

Prince William's younger brother is well known as a laidback and carefree Royal, happy to enjoy life as it comes as well as working hard for a selection of different charities.

The differences don't end there either.

While most of the Royal Family celebrated their first birthday with a mop of blonde hair, Prince Harry stands out as the only ginger-haired Prince in the family!

Say cheese!

Top: Prince Charles pictured on his first birthday with the future Queen Elizabeth and (right) his nanny

Above: Princess Elizabeth, who later became Queen, waves from a carriage in 1928

Prince Andrew at the age of one at
Euston Station in 1961

Prince Harry, aged one, with big brother William, Lady Davina Windsor,
Princess Diana and Princess Michael of Kent

Princess Anne sits on her
mother's knee on her first
birthday with big brother
Charles at her side

'Prince
George is
blond, bonny,
playful and
smiley. His
dad was the
same – and
so was his
grandad'

THE LAST
KING
George

King George VI (then known as Prince Albert) as a baby in 1895. He was crowned King (right) in 1937

Daily Mirror
THURSDAY, MAY 13, 1937

THE CROWNING OF GEORGE VI
KING AND EMPEROR

*W*hile all eyes are on the new Prince George – who is likely to one day become King George VII – we take a look at the last King George.

King George VI, Queen's Elizabeth II's father, only became the King due to the biggest crisis in the history of the British Monarchy.

In 1938, Prince Albert of York – or "Bertie" as he was more commonly known – was a happily married man with two daughters, Princess Elizabeth and Margaret.

He had no designs on the throne but unfortunately for him, neither did his brother, the then King Edward VIII.

Edward VIII was in a relationship with an American called Wallis Simpson who, having been divorced twice, could never become the Queen.

Edward had to pick the monarchy or Wallis. He chose Wallis and thrust his shy and stuttering brother onto the world stage.

However, rather than shrink from the task, George VI became a truly magnificent King, marshalling Britain through World War Two, conquering his speech impediment and stabilising the monarchy after its terrible recent upheaval.

He died in his sleep in 1952 following a prolonged period of illness. He deserved to be remembered as an unfailingly loyal and determined man who stepped into the breach when his country needed him the most.

If the current Prince George follows in his footsteps, the British monarchy is in very safe hands indeed.

King George VI with Prime Minister Neville Chamberlain in 1939

Growing up IN THE ROYAL SPOTLIGHT

Living life in the glare of the nation will be tough for George at times, but he doesn't have to look far for advice on how to cope with it...

They may not always like it but the unavoidable truth for the Royal Family is that they live their entire lives under the spotlight.

It cannot be easy to be constantly followed around by paparazzi and members of the press, keen for a quote and a headline and something to fill the next day's papers.

However, it comes with the territory and most of the time the Royal Family cope brilliantly with the interest in their lives.

Growing up is tough at the best of times and that is only exacerbated by the glare of the spotlight and Prince George is likely to feel that as much as anybody – particularly as he is also an heir to the throne.

Yet one bonus for Prince George is that he only has to look around him for hints, tips and advice for how to cope with the public's interest in him.

Every single member of his family, from his great-grandmother to his uncle Harry, have learnt how to cope with the situation.

The Queen's upbringing was actually very quiet because she was never expected to become the monarch.

It was only when her uncle, King Edward VIII, abdicated in 1938, that she moved up to heir to the throne as her father, King George VI, took over.

Until then, she had lived a relatively normal life alongside her sister Margaret.

However, her own children did not really enjoy the same privilege. Following his birth in 1948, interest in Prince Charles was immediate and overwhelming as newspapers wanted to know all about his life.

As he grew up, Charles found himself at the centre of plenty of public scrutiny, particularly when he attended Gordonstoun school in Scotland. Prince Charles hated the place and that made growing up there doubly hard.

His three siblings, Princess Anne, Prince Andrew and Prince Edward also had their fair share of ups and downs as they grew up, especially Prince Edward, who dropped out of Royal Marine training in 1987, much to the public's derision.

Daddy's life through a lens

Prince William's childhood was recorded at every stage whether he was...

cuddling Mummy...

dribbling...

flying...

being cheeky...

sheltering...

starting school...

looking sheepish...

pushing little brother around...

enjoying Christmas...

watching tennis...

relaxing with Dad...

or grieving...

Charles'
2nd birthday

Charles'
3rd birthday

Charles'
4th birthday

George's grandfather Prince Charles has also lived a life under the microscope as these pictures taken on his birthdays illustrate

All the main events in a Royal's life are documented by the media and by the public so christenings, first days at school, sporting achievements and any ups and downs are all events the outside world will take an interest in.

Prince William, who was intensely shy as a child before growing into the super-confident and mature man the public sees today, had to grimace his way through his opening day at Eton College in 1995 and it was the same when he went to the University of St. Andrew's in 2001.

He had also had his fair share of bumps and bruises by that point, especially back in 1991 when he was accidently whacked with a golf club. He had to undergo surgery for a depressed skull fracture at Great Ormond Street Hospital which has left him, in his own words, with a "Harry Potter-style" scar.

William's younger brother, Harry, is another who has spent his life under the glare but it is something he is now used to and he will pass his own perspective on to his first nephew.

He said: "I want to make sure he has a good upbringing, stays out of harm's way and has fun – the rest of it I will leave up to the parents!"

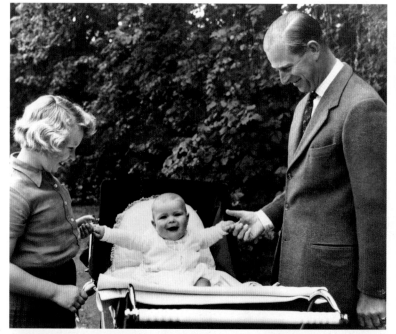

Prince Harry (right), aged four, dressed as a shepherd ahead of a nursery nativity play

Charles'
5th birthday

Charles'
6th birthday

Charles'
7th birthday

'Christenings, first days at school, sporting achievements and any ups and downs are all events the outside world will take an interest in'

Crash happy Harry!

Beginners' guide to nude gardening

RECLUSE LEAVES HIS NURSE £7m

By BOB WESTERDALE

Ferrari

Growing up in public

Far left above: **Prince Andrew with sister Anne and the Duke of Edinburgh in 1960**

Far left below: **Prince Harry waves from inside a car at Zurich Airport**

Left: **The Queen and Duke of Edinburgh – and a pet corgi – with all their children in Windsor**

Above: **A newspaper page from 1991 is an example of the interest shown in the Royal Family**

AUSTRALIA & NEW ZEALAND

THE FIRST

Big
HOLIDAY

George's first royal tour gave his parents the chance to really show him off. There are a few special snaps for the family album in here...

Kate, William and George arrive in
New Zealand to begin their tour

When Prince William and his wife Catherine, the Duchess of Cambridge, landed in New Zealand they prepared themselves on board so that they would look fresh and sharp after their 30-hour journey.

No Royal can afford to look tired or withdrawn, no matter how hard a long-haul flight is on the body and mind.

They need not have worried though because for the first time since they became a royal couple, all eyes were no longer on them.

They were on the young man being carried in his mother's arm. Prince George had well and truly arrived at the other end of the world.

Dressed in an all-cream ensemble, topped off by a cardigan, the young prince seemed to have coped well with the rigours of travelling so far and for so long.

Prince William and Catherine looked their usual dapper selves and would normally have stolen the headlines – but there was only one star on show on this occasion.

The royal threesome arrived in Wellington on April 7,

2014, as part of a three-week tour of New Zealand and Australia, one of the frequent worldwide trips that the Royal Family make to the various long-range parts of the Commonwealth.

New Zealand Prime Minister John Key was on hand to received his country's high-profile guests and he urged New Zealanders to show them the kind of welcome that his country is famous for.

Despite the grey and drizzly weather in Wellington, many did turn out to welcome the new visitors and they were then treated to a traditional Maori welcome.

After leaving the airport, they were taken to Government House, home of the Governor-General, for an official welcome ceremony, where children from a local school waved union flags at the entrance.

It was a low-key arrival, rather than an entrance filled with pomp and ceremony. However, it was enough to give New Zealand and the rest of the world a glimpse of the rapidly growing prince. And over the next few weeks, his popularity would only grow and grow...

Everyone is allowed a bad hair day when they're on holiday – and princes are no different! Here George is safe in Mummy's arms before his parents experienced a unique welcome to New Zealand (above)

TOUR ITINERARY

New Zealand

April 7 - Wellington: Arrive to ceremonial welcome.

April 8 - Rest.

April 9 - Wellington: Meet parents and their babies at Government House with George.

April 10 - Blenheim: Events to commemorate the 100th anniversary of the start of the First World War.
Wellington: State Reception where William will unveil a portrait of the Queen.

April 11 - Auckland: Meet serving air force personnel and their families. Race each other across Auckland Harbour in Team New Zealand Americas Cup yachts. Ride on a Sealegs craft - boat that can be driven into and out of water.

April 12 - Waikato: William views an aircraft factory while Kate goes to a children's hospice. Both travel through Hamilton town centre and meet Olympic athletes and open the new velodrome.

April 13 - Dunedin (Travel away from George for one night): Maori tribal welcome, visit cathedral then watch and participate in a Rippa Rugby tournament - non contact rugby.
Queenstown: Wine tasting, travel on the Shotover Jet - 50mph white water ride.

April 14 - Christchurch: Ceremony for those who died in 2011 earthquake. Watch a 2015 Cricket World Cup event, later visit air force museum and memorial wall.

April 15 - Rest.

April 16 - Wellington: Visit a police training college, sign the city's visitor book then depart for Australia.

PLAY TIME FOR PRINCE GEORGE

As first public engagements go, few other Royal Family members will beat it for originality – or noise.

On one hand, it was the most normal Wednesday morning in the world.

A gang of doting mums and dads, chasing their young children around as they played with toys, whimpered, screamed and ran around – the same as any other playgroup morning.

However, the presence of a blond-haired young man from England changed all that.

Because among the children present was the eight-month-old future King and his parents the Duke and Duchess of Cambridge.

The party, organised by the New Zealand child welfare charity Plunket at the Governor General's residence, Government House, in Wellington was a riot of colour, noise, celebration and laughter.

Prince George, completely unaware that the event was focused on him, did just as any other child would.

He rattled toys, played with teddy bears, clung closely to his mum and spent the time getting to know his newfound, tiny friends.

George wowed the room but his parents did not do too badly either, impressing the other parents present with their laidback manner –despite being sneezed on.

One baby spluttered and coughed all over the Duchess of Cambridge but she laughed it off as just one of those things that babies do.

The mortified mum, Vicky King, said: "I was holding my baby, Alton, and he sneezed because he has got a bit of a cold at the moment. She got a bit of a fright - she said 'Oh!'

"But they laughed, and I was okay about it, because even though she is royalty she is a mum too, and knows what it is like to have a baby. She took it all in her stride."

The laughs continued after the playgroup as Prince William joked that his son's size and wrestling skills – Prince George had done his best to swipe several toys from other children – meant he was going to be a natural sportsman.

In a speech following the royals' first full day of engagements on tour, the Duke said: "I hope that George doesn't keep you up!

"He's a bonny lad and you'll all be very pleased to know that he's currently preparing for life as a prop forward!"

TOUR ITINERARY
Australia

April 16 - Sydney: Arrive and attend reception at the Sydney Opera House.

April 17 - Sydney: Fire-ravaged street in Blue Mountains.

April 18 - Sydney: Attend the Royal Easter Show, visit a children's hospice before watching a demonstration by surf life-saving volunteers.

April 19 - Brisbane: RAF base visit then reception for Queensland's young people.

April 20 - Sydney: Cathedral service then visit Taronga Zoo where the bilby enclosure is being named after Prince George.

April 21 - Rest.

April 22 - Uluru (Ayres Rock) (Second night away from George): Visit the National Indigenous Training Academy, view Aboriginal art display then walk round part of the rock.

April 23 - Adelaide: View young people's music workshop and watch skateboarding display.

April 24 - Canberra: Visit the National Portrait Gallery, attend a reception at Parliament House, plant a tree at the National Arboretum.

April 25 - Canberra: Attend ANZAC Day March, lay a wreath and plant a 'Lone Pine' tree in the Memorial Garden. Depart for home.

The Duke and Duchess of Cambridge receive a personalised Australian cricket baggy green cap for their son

After the drab skies of New Zealand, the royal party travelled to the sunnier climes of Australia, landing in Sydney on April 16.

And Prince George was as acclaimed, feted and adored in Australia as he had been just across the Tasman Sea.

After arriving at Sydney Airport – where Kate carried a rather grumpy-looking Prince George off the plane – the royals headed to Circular Quay for an Opera House reception with 400 guests.

William quipped: "I should have brought my sunglasses", as they enjoyed warm sunshine following a tour of New Zealand blighted by rain.

Looking bright and breezy in a vibrant yellow dress – one of the colours of Australia – Kate waved to the crowds before disappearing inside the world-famous building.

Australia came to a standstill following their arrival and remained that way throughout the hugely successful second leg of the trip.

One of the Duke and Duchess of Cambridge's greatest and most popular traits are their comfortable and easy natures around people and they demonstrated that endlessly when in Australia.

They went from camping in the Outback to taking "selfies" with members of the public, proving beyond doubt that the heir to the throne and his wife are as 'normal' as any future monarch can be. All three of the royal party looked super relaxed throughout their adventure and Prince George again stole most of the headlines while Prince William repeatedly praised Australia and Australians.

"For Catherine, Harry and me, born in the early 80s, we've never known anything else - Australia and Australians have always been for us a beacon of confidence, creativity in the arts and sporting ability," he said.

And the royal visit got the biggest compliment possible from Australian Prime Minister Tony Abbott – who claimed that William, Catherine and Prince George were a bigger and more important star than Aussie surfing king Kelly Slater. In Australia, praise comes no higher than that!

William, Kate and George arrive in Sydney to begin the Australian leg of their tour

Snapped!

GEORGE FOLLOWS IN DAD'S FOOTSTEPS

With a dad, uncle and grandad all committed to helping save and preserve the world's wildlife, it comes as little surprise that Prince George also seems keen to help.

On his only official engagement in Australia, Prince George wowed crowds at Taronga Zoo in Sydney as he was introduced to a bilby – a rat-like marsupial – that had been named in his honour.

However, unlike his close family, the young prince has not yet quite mastered the art of animal conservation.

Because, when he came face-to-face with the bilby, he tried to almost rip its ear off!

Prince George's mum, who was carrying her son, said: "He's trying to grab his ear." And William added: "If he gets it he'll never let go," kissing the top of his son's head.

The young prince was clearly enthralled by the bilby that had originally been called 'Boy' until the Australian government donated £5,000 to Taronga Zoo's bilby preservation programme in honour of George's birth.

After meeting the bilby, William and Kate unveiled a plaque that read: "A national gift from the Commonwealth Government to commemorate the birth of His Royal Highness Prince George of Cambridge."

George's enthusiasm at meeting his namesake won hearts throughout the zoo. He definitely appeared to be a conservationist in the making and he certainly impressed Taronga Zoo's bilby expert, Paul Davies.

He said: "Prince George was absolutely fantastic. I've never seen a little boy quite so excited about meeting a bilby.

"He had his hands up on the glass of the exhibit and he was patting the glass.

"A big part of wildlife conservation is about raising awareness and today we've an opportunity to showcase the bilby not only to Australia, but to the world."

After visiting the bilby enclosure, George also attracted huge attention at the birds of prey exhibition and he again won a whole host of new friends. Bird keeper Brendan Host said: "They were very friendly. I think they enjoyed their experience and I definitely enjoyed meeting them. It was a wonderful chance to show the amazing diversity of wildlife we have in Australia."

Snapped!

OUT AND ABOUT DOWN UNDER

Although Prince George offered the 'box-office' headline of the latest royal visit Down Under, his parents also attracted huge attention and managed to cram in a variety of different, interesting events.

While Prince George's appearances were strictly rationed, William and Kate were anything but hidden away as they travelled throughout Oz in a bid to see as much of the country as possible.

Kate and William visited the Blue Mountains to meet families affected by devastating fires in October, 2013, and they also did plenty of sightseeing in the area.

Further trips followed to a lifesaving display in Manly, and a visit to the RAAF base at Amberley on a one-day trip to Brisbane.

The Royal couple also paid their respects to Australia's fallen troops as they attended the Dawn Service on Anzac Day at the Australian War Memorial.

Prince William, a keen sports fan, also got to meet Glenn McGrath, the legendary Australian fast bowler, who presented him with an iconic 'Baggy Green' cap, the famous headwear worn by Australia's Test cricketers.

However, the highlight of the trip was William and Kate's 'glamping' trip to the stunning and breathtaking Uluru rock where the royal couple were left in awe by Australia's astonishing beauty.

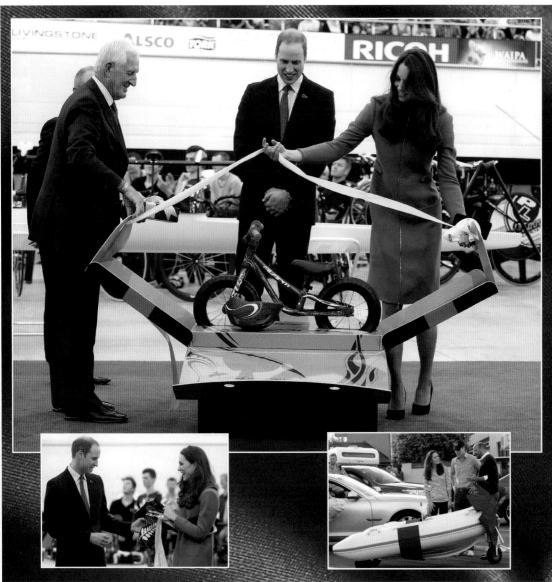

PRINCELY PRESENTS

It wasn't just goodwill that Prince George received while on tour in Australia and New Zealand. Here are some of the gifts he was lucky enough to get...

From New Zealand:
- Miniature Sealegs amphibious boat
- Avanti Lil Ripper bicycle and crash helmet
- A baby-sized cycling jersey with HRH Prince George on the back
- Child-sized flying helmet lined with possum fur

From Australia:
- Kangaroo backpack
- Giant cuddly wombat
- Customised surfboard
- Rocking horse
- Boomerang
- A stuffed bilby
- A yellow car sticker that reads "Wild Child on Board"
- Skateboard with "George" and two kangaroos painted on it

Seeing the sights, meeting the people

Anti-clockwise from top left:

Kate and William at Uluru (Ayres Rock)

The Duke and Duchess on the steps of Sydney Opera House

William meets Australian cricket legend Glenn McGrath

William talks to the people of Brisbane and (above) receives a surfboard on a visit to Manly beach, Sydney

Charming where Daddy has charmed before

The 2014 visit to Australia and New Zealand echoes a similar visit made by Prince William, with his parents Charles and Diana, when he was only nine months old in 1983...

Do we really have to go home now? George's face says it all as William and Kate bid a fond farewell to Australia after a successful 18-day tour

A Nation's PRIDE

From plastic lookalikes to special daffodils and re-named pubs – the demonstrations of affection for a popular prince just haven't stopped

The beaming wide smiles on the faces of Prince William and Kate Middleton as they stood on the steps of the Lindo Wing with their newborn son said it all.

They were a family who were ecstatic with their new arrival – the same feeling new mums and dads up and down the land get.

When both sets of grandparents arrived, those smiles grew even wider as Prince George began his charm offensive in style.

And while the birth of a happy, healthy baby is always a cause for celebration, it is fair to say that Prince George's arrival was greeted with more glee than usual.

In fact, every corner of the country queued up to celebrate his birth and the Royal Family's popularity seemed greater than ever.

All manner of different trinkets, gifts, presents and mementos were made to mark George's birth.

And Prince Charles also picked up a tenner on behalf of his new grandson!

While visiting the Royal Welsh Show just 36 hours after George's birth, royalist Amanda Winney, 49, gave the cash in a card so that William and Kate would buy a cuddly toy for their new son – and she was amazed when Prince Charles happily took the gift and promised her it would get to Prince George safely!

Schoolchildren across the country threw Union Flag-filled parties to celebrate Prince George's birth. Fetes and summer fairs that were already planned had an extra special and patriotic feel to them as the public cheered on the Royal Family and a whole range of plates, tea towels, cups and banners were made to celebrate the event.

Crowds gathering to see the easel at Buckingham Palace which announced Prince George's birth demonstrate the interest in the baby's life from day one

Congratulations!

Right: Royal fans react to George's birth outside the Lindo Wing of St Mary's Hospital

Below: Cards made by children at Bucklebury Church of England Primary School in the village the Middleton family are from

Bottom: Gifts left for baby George by well-wishers

Perhaps the most amazing gesture belongs to Terry Rigg, the landlord of The Sycamore pub in Watford.

After taking over at the pub, he decided he wanted to change its name so the pub was rechristened The Prince George.

He wrote to William and Kate to let them know about the name change and was astonished to open his mail one day to find that they had responded.

A letter from St. James's Palace said: "The Duke and Duchess were touched that you would change the name of your pub to The Prince George and have asked me to send you and your customers their warmest thanks and best wishes."

Mr Rigg added: "I was not expecting a reply and we were thrilled to receive the letter and photo of the young family."

The country's politicians also got in on the act and sent their presents to Buckingham Palace for the new family.

Prime Minister David Cameron sent a set of Roald Dahl books, Labour leader Ed Miliband sent an apple tree to be planted while Liberal Democrat leader and Deputy Prime Minister Nick Clegg sent an embroidered blanket and – thoughtfully – some super-strength coffee to help the new parents cope.

Mr Clegg said: "We have thrown in with the gift a large bag of our favourite coffee because, as parents of young boys, we know you need coffee when you are coping with little boys."

If the presents given to Prince George in Great Britain have not been weird and wonderful enough, on the recent tour of Australia and New Zealand, the young prince got a huge selection of new toys to play with.

In New Zealand he picked up an Avanti Lil Ripper bicycle and crash helmet, a baby-sized cycling jersey with HRH Prince George on the back, a child-sized flying helmet lined with possum fur and the gifts continued Down Under as he got a kangaroo backpack, a giant cuddly wombat, a customised surfboard, a rocking horse, a boomerang, a stuffed bilby and a skateboard.

George seemed to love all his presents but his dad confirmed that one had pleased him more than any other.

In his farewell speech, delivered at Parliament House in Canberra, Prince William said: "We go away with wonderful memories, and George goes away with his cuddly wombat, which he has taken to chewing so lovingly."

CONGRATULATIONS
Will & Kate
on the birth of your baby son
LOVE FROM US ALL AT THE COTTAGE INN
22 /JULY / 2013

Town crier Tony Appleton lets everyone at St Mary's Hospital know about the happy event

'The Duke and Duchess were touched that you would change the name of your pub and have asked me to send you their warmest thanks'

Georgie Boy

Fragrant Rose

Paperwhite

Some Georgie Boy daffodils, named in Prince George's honour, are displayed at the Chelsea Flower Show

Could you give this to George please?

Above: **Kate receives a baby grow for George from Aaron Russell-Andrews and daughter Teegan**

Right: **A baby boy balloon in the crowd**

Next right: **Prince William receives gifts to pass on to George – a toy motorbike and a teddy bear**

Far right: **Even Grandad is asked to pass on gifts as Prince Charles receives a cuddly toy for George**

Prince George wasn't the only baby born on July 22nd, 2013. Here are six mums, pictured with their newborns, who knew what the Duchess of Cambridge felt like that day, while Ella Kate (inset) was born just four minutes after the royal baby.

This is Marion Foster who made this child-sized kilt for Prince George. It is made of Strathearn tartan and was presented to William to pass on to his son.

This polo playing Prince George doll is one of only three made by Zapf Creations. One of them was sent directly to the Duke and Duchess of Cambridge. This doll was given to Kate Middleton lookalike Heidi Agan.

An advanced, bonny Winston Churchill lookalike!

And here are some of the other things people have said about George in the past year...

DUKE OF CAMBRIDGE:
"He's a little bit of a rascal. He either reminds me of my brother or me when I was younger, I'm not sure, but he's doing very well at the moment."

DUCHESS OF CAMBRIDGE (on the tour of New Zealand and Australia):
"He's been changing so much while we've been away."

SHELLEY HORTON (Australian TV presenter):
"I think he (George) is a republican slayer. He is just so cute and William and Kate are such a lovely couple."

DUKE OF CAMBRIDGE (on leaving Australia):
"We go away with wonderful memories, and George goes away with his cuddly wombat, which he has taken to chewing so lovingly."

Zara Phillips and Mike Tindall – parents of Mia

DUKE OF CAMBRIDGE (in Australia):
"Catherine and I were very grateful for the kind messages and gifts from across the country when George was born.

"I suspect George's first word might be 'bilby' – only because 'koala' is harder to say. We really look forward to our time here together as a family."

**ANTONIA MILNER
(Australian paediatrician):**
"He looks like a mobile baby who actively plays with toys and crawls around and he could be almost walking which is very good at nine months.

"But getting excited with the little animal in the zoo, that's pretty advanced. [The Duke and Duchess] do have a pet dog, I know that, so he might have experience with animals.

"He's obviously aware of the world and interested in the world. It's lovely to see such an aware baby."

DUKE OF CAMBRIDGE (in New Zealand):
"George is a bonny lad. You'll be pleased to know that he's currently preparing for life as a prop forward.

"I hope that George doesn't keep you up! He's at his most vocal at 3am, as you may have noticed. I swear I heard him doing the haka this morning."

OLYMPIC SAILOR BEN AINSLIE:
"The Duchess was very keen (for George to go sailing) but not for a couple of years yet — when he's about 7 or 8. But we'd love to get the Duchess sailing sooner. She's very keen and of course we'd love to get her out on the water — she doesn't get to do it much now."

**DUKE OF CAMBRIDGE
(on Christmas Day 2013):**
"We've had a good morning with George and I can't wait until next year when he's bigger."

PRINCE HARRY:
"He's growing up. He is walking, and he has big, chubby cheeks. He looks like a young Winston Churchill."

MIKE TINDALL (on his daughter meeting George for the first time):
"I don't think Mia will remember that day, she was two months old, but it was great, it was carnage. George was eating at the time. He'd got to that stage where more food goes on the table than in his mouth."

DUKE OF CAMBRIDGE:
"As you might have gathered, Catherine and I have recently become proud parents - of a baby who has a voice to match any lion's roar!"

PRINCE HARRY:
"It's fantastic to have another addition to the family. I only hope my brother knows how expensive my babysitting charges are."

*William and Kate on
Christmas Day – after having
a good morning with George*

WHAT NEXT FOR THE *Growing Prince?*

Prince William pictured taking part in his school sports day in 1988 at Richmond Sports Stadium

So then, what next for Prince George? In what direction will his life go?

And as he waits to take over as King from his father, Prince William, what is George likely to do with his royal time?

As the third in line to the English throne, responsibilities and a life in the full glare of the public is inevitable.

Although George's parents have made a concerted effort – and promises – to ensure their son's upbringing is as normal as possible, Prince George's position in the Royal Family will ensure that his life will be anything but conventional.

He is likely to attend one of Britain's best public schools and Eton College will be the favourite choice, particularly as William attended there. However, Winchester College, Marlborough College, Wellington College or Harrow School may also fit the bill, particularly if Kate and William decide that they do not wish George to follow an identical route through life as his father.

And just like William's own first day at school, as well as landmark days along the way like sports days and receiving exam results, George is likely to be pictured as often as the media are allowed to and be the subject of much interest.

Prince William is immensely proud of his own work in the Armed Forces with the Household Cavalry and it would be no surprise if George also ended up taking a military path.

However, again, there will be no pressure on the young Prince to conform or live up to what his father has done – William and Kate want to bring up a healthy, happy, well-adjusted young man and they want to keep the pressures of Kingship off his young shoulders for as long as possible.

In other words, they want the same as every other set of loving, doting parents – they simply want the best for their son, regardless of his future role in national and international life.

George's protective parents will do their best to give their son a 'normal' life

HRH Prince George of Cambridge